the original Gamedrive

Gerald Hinde

To my wife Pam:
'The world and all that is in it
belong to the Lord;
The earth and all who live on it
are his.' Psalm 24:1

First Edition

Copyright © 1989 by Gerald Hinde

Produced by
Gerald Hinde Productions

First Published in 1989 by
Gerald Hinde Productions

ISBN: 0 620 13365 1

Designed by Tim Rowland
Photographed & written by Gerald Hinde

Printed by Interpak
Reproduction by Hirt & Carter

Contents

Introduction 7

Abandoned Leopard Cub 27

Night of Terror 39

Giraffe Kill 47

Sunrise Sunset 59

Newborn Cubs 71

Leopard 85

Savuti 97

Return to Savuti 117

Etosha Pan 135

Death of a Cub 149

Sharp eyes scanning, this pied kingfisher hovers above the water, ready to plummet in pursuit of a meal.

Foreword

Reflect for a moment on an extract from the words of a great visionary, Chief Seattle, when he wrote a letter to the President of the United States (1864) ... "For when all the animals are gone — man will die of a great loneliness of spirit" ...

For many years Gerald Hinde has been a regular visitor at the Londolozi Game Reserve. I have been privileged to witness the transformation of a person who 'initially' had a mild interest in wildlife, to one who has now become deeply involved in wildlife conservation. I personally believe that this book will make a significant contribution to the massive environmental awareness now taking place amongst people around the globe. The appeal of this book is that it enlightens the reader on the simple beauty and the stark reality of wildlife. This book will help us to reconcile ourselves to the fact that we share this planet with other creatures, that these wild animals have a right to exist, and that they can contribute to our quality of life, offering enormous enjoyment and benefit to millions of people. Only when we have grasped this fact will we have made our first tentative step towards ensuring our own long term survival.

I salute you, Gerald, for a fine effort. I welcome you aboard as you make your contribution to environmental awareness, and I challenge others who are in a position of influence, to look at their situation and ask themselves: "Can we afford to allow the existing environmental trends to persist? What contribution can I make to a better world?"

Dave Varty

Introduction

I am not quite sure which came first, my love for wildlife or my intense interest in photography. The two passions have developed virtually in tandem over the years to give me infinite enjoyment and enormous physical and spiritual fulfillment. Certainly, a fruitful school for both interests has been years of steady exposure to the African bushveld.

It all started some 35 years ago when I was 9. My parents took me to the Kruger National Park and from that time the bush has attracted me like a magnet, pulling me back time and time again to enjoy unique experiences with animals in their natural habitat.

It was natural to develop my enthusiastic, beginner's interest in photography into an enjoyable, practical hobby that allowed me to record my experiences in the bush. These visual records fit together in a jig-saw of memories to give me hours of pleasure during which I can relax from the harsh realities of my work-a-day world.

... Introduction contd.

My first introduction to photography was by way of an 8mm cine camera. My father was the cameraman and I was an eager, if inexperienced, assistant. Our first wildlife adventure movie ran for a full 15 minutes and even included a lion kill. In those days, lion used to hunt alongside the Sabie River road using passing cars as cover. We certainly saw our fair share of lion-at-prey on our annual visits to the Kruger National Park.

From our humble 8mm movie camera we graduated to a 16mm Paillard Bolex. With this much more sophisticated piece of equipment my father managed to make an award-winning wildlife film. However, he subsequently lost interest in photography, and I inherited both his role of 'Chief Photographer' and his camera.

My ambition to become a game ranger was never realised, and I inevitably joined the family motor business with which I am still deeply involved. As the years passed and the pressures of a growing business intensified, the natural untainted order of the bushveld drew me back time and again.

As I became more and more involved with the bush, spending as much time as possible pursuing my interest, I changed the méthod through which I recorded my experiences to 35mm still photography. Not only was this more convenient and adaptable in application, it made it easier to enjoy my constantly expanding photogaphic record. During these years I was privileged to visit many game parks, all the time increasing my enjoyment and understanding of wildlife.

Predators are seen as cold-blooded killers by many people, but surely the predator is an essential part of the ecology, killing only in order to survive.

Five years ago I started to visit the Londolozi Game Reserve and my subsequent experiences in that 'wildlife paradise' inspired me to publish this book. During these five years, I have studied conservation, learning a great deal about it from highly dedicated conservationists.

'Gamedrive' is based on my personal observations and experiences on numerous game drives, but it would not have been possible to gather this material without the help of rangers, game-farm owners and many other good folk involved with conservation in one way or another. I thank them all for their encouragement, assistance and patience, without which my nerve and enthusiasm may well have failed me!

My love for predators and my involvement with them is the main theme of this book. Such is my absorption with predators, that efforts by many people to turn my interests elsewhere have, by and large, proved unsuccessful. Although all aspects of nature continually interest me, I am irresistably drawn to predators, and become totally absorbed by the sharply-etched moments of drama that are an essential part of their life in the wild. Sharp contrast indeed with the lazy, unfulfilled life of the predator in captivity.

Predators are seen as cold-blooded killers by many people, but surely the predator is an essential part of the ecology, killing only in order to survive. Even when a leopard kills twice or more within a short period of time, it is merely because the leopard is an excellent

... Introduction contd.

provider, and uses suitable opportunities to store food against the distinct possibility of leaner times. Predators naturally dispose of weak, diseased animals, allowing stronger animals to breed, thus ensuring the survival of the species.

Man inhibits the natural movements of wild animals by fencing them in, and by constantly appropriating land for his own needs. Restricting the natural movements of animals causes considerable suffering, and for some, an untimely death. Numbers diminish and some species face extinction as man encroaches upon more and more natural environments.

There are those who unremittingly strive to preserve the natural environment of our beautiful land, and as a dedicated conservationist I salute you all who work in this worthwhile cause. Through the endeavours of a pitiably small minority, our children may yet enjoy a little of what we have enjoyed — the 'real Africa'. To those intent on destroying the wonderful natural assets of our land, I say 'Stop! You have gone far enough. Leave what remains of God's most precious gifts of nature for future generations to enjoy.'

Let us teach those who have traditionally lived by hunting, but are now forced to break the law by poaching, that conservation will help to meet their needs. Conservation will generate tourism, and tourism will open up job opportunities.

I am fortunate to have studied the wildlife of our country and to have obtained photographs that are dramatic and informative, and will give enjoyment to many people. The photographs in this book are of the animals in their most compromising situations, with some of the incidents that I have described happening in thick bush or at a distance that made photography impractical. Possibly the many photographs that I have filed away or rejected would give a more complete picture of the predator — obscured in thickets, living in a secret world of his own. Unfortunately that would take up many times more space than I have available and therefore, I have had to be highly selective.

Interaction between predator and prey occurs mainly at night, which makes recording this dramatic aspect of wildlife most difficult. Although modern cameras, telephoto lenses and film make it possible to photograph wildlife far more easily than was possible a few years ago, so much takes place that is beyond the photographer's control. Fortunately anticipation, good judgment and considerable luck sometimes coincide, and we are privileged to record a few of the many exciting moments that happen naturally in the unspoilt regions of Africa.

In my quest to gather as much interesting material as possible, I have visited Etosha, the Kalahari Gemsbok Park, the Kruger National Park, Sabie Sand, Savuti and Timbavati. All these areas are different and have their own characteristic beauty. But from the

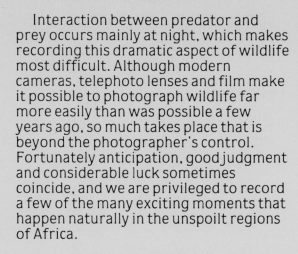

...Introduction contd.

bushveld areas of the Sabie Sand and Timbavati, to the desert areas of the Kalahari and dry, harsh Etosha, they have one feature in common — they provide a protected natural habitation for a large variety of wildlife.

I was always driven by the same urgency to photograph the action-packed moments generated by the wildlife with which I made contact. The long hours of waiting were sometimes frustratingly unproductive as the contact with my quarry would be all too brief, or at times disappointing, as I was unable to obtain an advantageous position to capture the culminating point of action on film. I find it hard to believe that anyone can have contact with wildlife in natural habitats, experience the cooling-down of a new day in the bush, or marvel at the fiery splendour of an African sunset, without knowing that these wonders are created by an Almighty power.

Genesis 1:24 'Then God said "Let the earth bring forth the living creatures according to its kind, cattle and creeping things and beasts of the earth, each according to its kind", and it was so. And God saw that it was good.'
Certainly my experiences in the African bush have led me to a belief in God as a wonderfully good and generous creator of all things.

Lions invariably settle down to sleep heavily for hours at a time after a good meal. They gorge themselves to repletion, instinctively providing against leaner periods.

The inquisitive look and playful antics of this young male leopard reminded me of a juvenile delinquent.

The spots on the shoulders, body and quarters are set more widely apart in symmetrical rows and combine in rosette-like clusters.

People tend to be nervous when being glared at by the amber-eyed stare of a lion.

Later that evening this lioness was instrumental in a zebra kill.

15

Sub-adult lions often become nomadic and may only become territorial at five or six years of age when they are strong enough to defend a territory.

Impala lambs often remain in 'crèche' groups within the herd but may become temporarily separated at times.

The average rhinoceros is a mixture of timidity, inquisitiveness, pugnacity and nervous irritability.

Lionesses are responsible for most of the hunting within the nucleus of the pride.

Lions are the most sociable of the cat family, associating in prides which may consist of a dominant male and other lions of all ages and sexes.

Wildebeest are very inquisitive and will stand staring at an intruder, continuously snorting. Finally they depart at a hunched, prancing gait, tails whisking wildly and heads down.

20

Cheetah are largely diurnal and will usually hunt in the early morning or late afternoon.

For fear of losing their kill to other predators they, are nervous, hurried feeders.

21

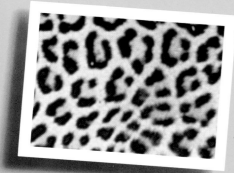

I have been privileged to watch and study the
mother leopard from close quarters over the past
five years. This has given me more of an indepth
knowledge about their secret lives.

Scentmarking, roaring and patrolling ensure that the pride's territory is not violated.

I followed these three-year-old lions for a period of ten days and found them to be proficient hunters.

Although lions often climb trees they are cumbersome and not at home in this environment.

The sub-adult cheetah pictured here with its mother is the surviving one of a litter of five. The other four were killed by lions at seven weeks.

Abandoned Leopard Cub

Many years have passed since my first game drive and in this time I have developed an ever-increasing respect for the animals, game rangers and not least of all , the trackers. Although the naïvety with which I initially approached the bush and its inhabitants has turned into a cautious respect, the excitement and thrill each time we set out on a game drive will never leave me.

Each drive is unique, and generates a special set of memories to store away and relive when the hustle and bustle of city life threaten to overwhelm my priorities. In a way, you could liken my experiences in the bush to the oasis on a desert journey. Just when my thirst for the wonderful peace of the bush becomes unbearable, an opportunity will arise for me once more to drink in the great thirst-quenching gifts of nature.

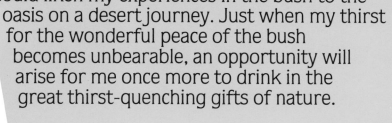

...Abandoned leopoard cub contd.

A game drive that we often recall around the campfire is one on which I saw a young leopard not long after it was abandoned by its mother. The morning had started typically enough. Hot coffee and rusks were somewhat sleepily consumed at five-thirty, our group subdued after a late evening of imbibing and swopping stories around the fire.

The cool morning air was refreshing, and we slowly came to life as the drive got under way. I was quite determined to find the young leopard.

The leopard we were seeking had become a firm favourite with rangers and trackers in the area. Abandoned by his mother at the age of ten months, the youngster had been left to fend for himself. Leopard cubs are usually separated from their mothers when they are approximately fourteen months old. The period between ten and fourteen months is when the mother passes on to the cub most of the skills and methods of hunting that it will need to survive. Unfortunately our young friend did not enjoy this advantage.

The radio crackled to life in our vehicle to tell us that the leopard had been spotted strolling along a dry river bed a few kilometres south of our present position.

For days the locals had been watching anxiously as the young leopard struggled against a somewhat unnatural killer — mange. Just as man can die from a heart attack brought on by stress, so this beautiful creature struggled against mange, caused by the stress of being unprepared to survive by himself in his own environment.

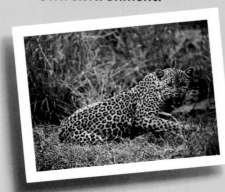

Just as man can die from a heart attack brought on by stress, so this beautiful creature struggled against mange, caused by the stress of being unprepared to survive by himself in his own environment.

This particular leopard was lucky enough to recover from this parasitic disease, which in most cases leads to an agonising death.

Taking the vehicle down an incline of about fourty-five degrees, we descended to the river bed and found the young leopard sitting quietly at the bottom of a tree. As I looked at this magnificent animal it was easy to see how, in his efforts to survive, he had captured the hearts of all who had been privileged to observe him.

Animals are much like humans. Each one has its own characteristics and personality, a fact that is difficult to discern when viewing animals in the inhibiting environment of captivity. As I sat and watched the behaviour of this young male, his inquisitive looks and playful antics, he reminded me of a juvenile delinquent. He was boisterous, cheeky and totally oblivious to the dangers of the world through being denied the disciplines learned under parental influence. You will meet this young leopard again in this book, and if I refer to him as the 'juvenile delinquent,' it is simply to remind you of his background so that you can more readily understand his actions.

Soon the young leopard decided to move on, and we followed him until he reached the road. Suddenly he was confronted by an older male leopard. A swift clip from the upraised paw of the adult warned the youngster to stay away and had him beating a hasty retreat. Some fifteen minutes later our young friend was confronted by five lions who sent him scrambling up a large marula tree. He climbed to the upper-most branches and remained there for the rest of the morning.

...Abandoned leopoard cub contd.

We learned later that the mother leopard was once again expecting cubs, this being her reason for abandoning the young male three weeks earlier. As I sat watching the young leopard, I reflected on an encounter with him that we experienced when he was seven months old. We had been following the mother and cub for some time that particular morning. As we rounded a bend in the road, the young leopard charged after a Swainson's Francolin who flew into a tree out of his reach.

As if to help her son, the mother leapt into the tree, caught the Francolin between her front paws, and descended graciously, presenting it alive to her cub. The delighted youngster proceeded to play with the bird, which promptly flew under our vehicle. Undeterred by the motorised presence, he gave chase, extracted the bird from its hiding place and proceeded to play with it much like an overgrown kitten would do. This was too much for the mother, who had been looking on with contempt. She snatched the bird from her son and swiftly killed it.

The youngster, disapproving of this maternal interference, tried to wrest the bird from her mother. Predictably, a good hiding was the result. The mother leapt on him, bit him, and vociferously made her feelings known. Such was the cheeky nature of the young leopard that, having recovered from his mother's

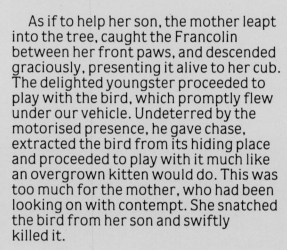

This was too much for the mother, who had been looking on with contempt. She snatched the bird from her son and swiftly killed it.

initial wrath, he walked up to her and snatched the bird away. This time, as much as a human mother might give in to a tiresome child, she let him do so without resistance. Our feelings were similar to the joy that one experiences when watching small children at play. However, we were all keenly aware that the young male would have to sharpen his hunting skills if he were to survive alone in the bush.

After he had finished his tasty morsel, the young leopard lay up in front of his mother who snarled angrily at him. We had noticed that she was short tempered with him of late, possibly because her age was beginning to rob her of her patience. In our estimation she was between 14 and 15 years of age, and although longevity is given at 20 years, this can vary from one area to another. She had recently lost one of her canine teeth, and this in the long term could prove to be a handicap.

Leopard cubs are usually dependent on their mothers until the age of 14 – 18 months, whereafter they are left to fend for themselves.

As a result of its secretive and shy nature, its nocturnal and solitary disposition, the leopard has a wider distribution than any of the larger cats.

When hunting, leopard frequently climb trees from which they can survey the surrounding countryside.

ABANDONED LEOPARD CUB

The young male leopard had been abandoned by his mother at the tender age of ten months. On this occasion he had been chased up a tree by lions.

The young leopard's sister had been killed by lions when only a few weeks old. With no companionship he sought constant attention from his mother which resulted in her being short tempered with him.

The mother leopard had lost one canine at approximately 14 years of age but this, as yet, had not become a handicap.

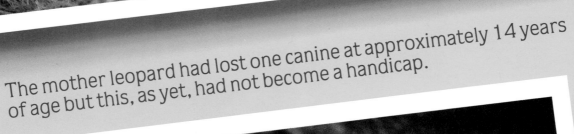

As the name suggests, waterbuck are often found near water and may immediately make for the water when threatened by predators.

Night of Terror

On one trip to a private game park in the Eastern Transvaal, I was accompanied by my parents, Pat and May Hinde and cousins, Muriel and Stan Webber.

An evening drive started off extremely well. Soon after sunset we came upon a pride of eight lions killing a porcupine. Some 20 minutes later they killed a kudu bull. Just after witnessing this impressive natural drama, a pair· of mating lions were discovered very near our camp. On our way to view this undisguised display of intimacy, we passed a lone buffalo bull standing in the road a mere twenty metres from the main camp. Had we known that this particular bull was to be the cause of a night of terror, we would most certainly have looked upon him with deep misgiving, if not outright fear. As it was, we merely noted his presence in the gathering dusk.

... Night of terror contd.

After watching the amorous lion and lioness for a while, we returned to camp at about 8.30 pm. As we approached our chalet, we heard a grunt which sounded very much like a lion. My first thought was that the mating lions had strayed into the camp and were now located between our chalets. I was wrong about the species, but not about the location. From out of the dark the buffalo charged us, goring my mother in the left thigh. She was thrown in the air by the upward thrust of the buffalo's horns and landed flat on her face screaming "Oh God — no". The buffalo swiftly turned, renewing his attack on my mother, straddling her in typical fashion. He went down on his front knees enabling him to crush her with the boss of his horns.

Everyone reacted spontaneously, but quite differently. Muriel, my cousin, ran towards the car park to call Warren, our game ranger. I ran towards the buffalo, hitting it with my camera case, and eventually grabbed the beast's left horn in an attempt to distract its attention. Dad, at this point, leaped at the buffalo from the front, literally taking the 'bull by the horns' and diverting the attack from my mother to himself. The buffalo plunged forwards with my father holding desperately onto his horns. Stopping short after a few metres, the powerful animal lowered his head, shaking it from side to side, trying to loosen dad's grip, but he held on determined to wrestle with the buffalo to the end.

The buffalo swiftly turned, renewing his attack on mother, his horns straddling her back in typical fashion. Then he went down on his front knees to crush her with the boss of his horns.

Fortunately, trouble with our spotlight during the evening drive had kept Warren in the camp trying to effect repairs. He grabbed his rifle in answer to our calls, and swiftly came to the rescue. Shooting at the buffalo, Warren killed it with the third bullet. The great bull collapsed to the ground, almost on top of my exhausted father.

My mother was rushed to the Skukuza doctor who cleaned her wound, started a drain, and treated her for shock.

Thanks to my father's spontaneous and extremely brave action a great tragedy in our family was avoided.

The terrifying ordeal had a wonderful side to it. At the time, my father was suffering from a serious condition called polymyalgia rheumatica (rheumatism of the blood), and was being treated with massive doses of cortizone. Incredibly, the shock produced increased adrenalin flow in the body and to this day he enjoys good health.

The lion pride had caught a porcupine and quills were embedded in their legs, throats, chests and faces. The meat was enjoyed by only a few of the lions while the others spent some time removing quills.

Buffalo are the most formidable of African big game and a lone bull was the cause of a night of terror for our family.

Buffalo often wallow in water in the heat of the day to keep cool.

Baboon are omnivorous, although largely vegetarian, feeding on wild fruit, berries, leaves, grasses, roots as well as a variety of insects, scorpions and lizards. Instances of baboons killing and feeding on new-born antelope lambs have been recorded.

Their regular companions, the oxpeckers, give buffalo some protection from the many parasites which infest them.

Young baboons are lovable bundles of energy who play together for hours.

GiraffeKill

On one never-to-be-forgotten drive, I was witness to the most awesome lion kill I have ever seen. During the afternoon we located a pride of two lionesses and two lions at Rhino Dam. They were extremely active, and provided us with some excellent viewing.

We had sundowners at the dam and enjoyed a particularly beautiful sunset. The orange-red sun pierced the clouds, sending streams of rays up into the heavens.

As the last sounds of the birds died down there was a momentary silence, then a noisy chorus of frogs began to serenade us. The calls of the owls and the nightjars were rudely interrupted by the four lions moving off, and the drama of the hunt began.

...Giraffe kill contd.

As the lions entered a thickly bushed, rocky area, they passed through a dry river bed which was extremely deep. We decided to follow, as by-passing would have meant a five kilometre journey. We pushed on regardless, but when we got near the bottom we came to a grinding halt, firmly lodged on huge boulders.

For the next hour, we dug boulders, and rolled them out of the way by using jack handles, tyre levers, wheel spanners and our feet and hands. Unloading the camera equipment for fear that it might be damaged if the vehicle toppled, we man-handled the vehicle out of its rock-bound situation.

While we wrestled with our rocky problems, the lions had moved on some distance, and it took a while for us to re-locate them. We came upon them eventually while they were assessing the possibilities of a herd of impala. Unsuccessful, they moved on, continuing the hunt.

We kept up with the lions, our spotlights catching the reflection of eyes glowing in the distance. As always during a hunt we cut the lights so as not to influence the situation in any way.

Soon, aided by the full moon, we were able to make out the forms of a giraffe and her youngster. They were walking nonchalantly away from the lionesses, totally oblivious of the impending danger.

The lionesses moved to within twenty-five metres of the giraffe before the giraffe became aware of them. As the lionesses covered the ground, the mother giraffe broke away to the right

At that moment, the mother giraffe ran into the fray to try and save her offspring. She desperately lashed out at the lions with her front feet, causing them to scatter.

causing her to be separated from her youngster. This normally spells doom for the inexperienced animal, and this situation was to be no different.

The lionesses brought the young animal down and were immediately joined by the males. At that moment, the mother giraffe ran into the fray to try and save her offspring. She desperately lashed out at the lions with her front feet, causing them to scatter. The lions regrouped and then drove the mother giraffe off. In the time that this took, the young giraffe had managed to raise himself, but his hip had been damaged and he could only walk with difficulty.

The lions seemed disorientated after chasing the mother, and they ran in various directions trying to locate the hapless youngster. After a short while the two males spotted the youngster, rapidly closed in, and brought it down, the one lion taking the giraffe by the throat in a strangle-grip. Once the giraffe was on the ground, the lion released his grip on its throat and they all lay with their forepaws pinning the giraffe down.

At this stage the lions had expended a tremendous amount of energy, and made no attempt to kill or eat the giraffe for some minutes. Finally the messy business of eating began, but unfortunately they did not continue with strangulation, and it took some time for the giraffe to die.

The aggression during the eating continued for two hours by which time the lions managed to finish off the whole carcass.

... Giraffe kill contd.

During this high drama, we were so busy taking photographs that we failed to realise that the battery of our vehicle had run down. Our attempts to radio camp were unsuccessful. Peter and Yvonne, our hosts, were having dinner at another camp, and we eventually managed to contact them at about 11:30 pm. They immediately set out for our position. The process of discovering our problem and contacting Peter and Yvonne took about half an hour. In this time our battery had run so flat that we could only hear them over our radio, but we were unable to transmit.

We eventually managed to communicate with them by using the microphone to create our own dubious method of morse code — one click for 'yes' and two clicks for 'no'. A typical message went like this:

"Are we on the right road?" — (we did not know where they were) — silence from us.
"Can you hear us" — one click from us.
"Are we on the right road?" — silence.
"Can you hear us?" — one click.
"Oh, you don't know where we are" — one click.
"Click three times when you have the lights in sight".
Five minutes later THREE CLICKS.

At this stage I repeatedly lit up the tree tops with my camera's flash equipment so that they could locate us as we were in deep bush, far from the nearest road.

After a thoroughly absorbing action-packed night we made it back to camp around 1:30 am and enjoyed supper (or was it breakfast) in the boma.

Lions' attitudes are in contrast to their reputation as 'King of the beasts', for they lie around in undignified postures for long periods.

Lion prides may split up into groups which tend to operate in different parts of the territory.

The huge canines are adapted to the holding of heavy prey and the delivery of the strangulation bite.

Flesh from the bones of prey is rasped off with the rough surface of the tongue.
Lions tend to avoid encounters where they can, relying on roaring, scent marking and patrolling to ensure that their territory is not violated.

The lion is the largest of the predators standing up to 1,25 metres at the shoulder and having a mass of up to 238 kg.

Where water is available, they will drink regularly, but they are not dependent on this and can subsist for long periods, getting their moisture requirements from their prey.

When the young giraffe split from its mother during the chase, we instinctively realised that it was doomed.

Lions hunt predominantly at night and are much more successful when a hunt is joined by all members of the pride.
The hunt and kill was filled with drama and terror. That night will live in my memory forever.

It took the four lions two hours to consume the entire carcass.

Lions have a quick digestive process and are able to take a second meal not long after gorging themselves.

Sunrise Sunset

Sunrise in the bushveld is a unique experience.

In the distance a lion roars, and nearby another answers — proclamation of territory. As the sun brings the faint orange glow to the horizon, the birds begin their own melodies. Guinea-fowl, bulbul, shrikes, weavers, barbets, starlings, louries and many others vocalise in unison. The calls of birds and animals are our signal to drive into African bushveld in order to experience the thrill of another game drive.

We passed herd animals enjoying both the faint chill of the morning air and the first rays of sunlight that bring relief from the dark shadows and lurking dangers of the night. Rounding a bend brought into view a group of rhino who lifted their heads at our approach, then relaxed and continued grazing.

... Sunrise, sunset contd.

Unlike his cousin the black rhino, whose numbers have almost dwindled to extinction, the numbers of white rhino have greatly increased as a result of conservation efforts. Annually, rhino are poached for their horns which, in the East, fetch higher prices per kilogram than gold. The horns are used for their fever-repressant qualities, or the still unproven attributes of an aphrodisiac. Horns, too, find their way to the Yemen Arab Republic where they are used to make highly prestigious dagger handles. It is deplorable that a species that has survived since time immemorial now faces extinction because of man's greed.

We approached the Sand River where, to our delight, we found hippo. These huge barrel-shaped amphibians with their short, stumpy legs, were lazing in the cool waters. We chuckled as the red billed ox-peckers landed on the hippos' backs and then, as the great animals submerged, quickly darted away to avoid a wetting.

We drove on until eleven o'clock that morning, when we were lucky to find the female leopard hunting along the dry river bed.

She was in an unusually hurried mood, and this impatience caused her to miss two consecutive attempts on duiker. At midday she moved to the southern bank of the river bed to stalk a herd of impala. We watched as she ran along the embankment towards

She managed to stay out of the view of the impala until the last moment, when with a sudden rush down the bank, she collided with a large impala ewe.

her prey. She managed to stay out of the view of the impala until the last moment, when with a sudden rush down the bank, she collided with a large impala ewe. Quickly and precisely the impala was grasped by the throat, and held in a strangulation-grip. The prey died less than five minutes later, and exhausted by the rush of the kill, the leopardess left the carcass in the river bed and moved a little distance off to rest in the shade of a strangler fig tree.

Normally, leopard will hoist their kill into a tree for safekeeping. On this occasion the leopardess had postponed this precaution, and later that afternoon radio contact with another vehicle told us that hyena had discovered the carcass of the impala ewe, and feasted until there were not even pickings for the vultures.

Sunset fell. Earlier that afternoon we had come across four lions resting at a waterhole. Now sunset prompted them to action, and they set out east across the clearing on the start of the hunt. Their first encounter occurred approximately one kilometre off. A lioness stopped, sniffed the air, then ran some one hundred and fifty metres towards a lone marula tree. A leopard, abandoning a duiker carcass hastily leapt from the tree and headed for the woodland. The lioness gave chase but could not match the speed of the leopard.

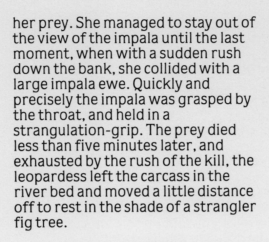

... Sunrise, sunset contd.

The lions regrouped under the tree and ran back and forth trying to locate the duiker carcass. Eventually a lioness spotted the meat in the tree and attempted, without success, to climb up. This ungainly action was followed by equally clumsy attempts by the two young lions. Eventually the second lioness succeeded, and tried to free the carcass which the leopardess had expertly lodged in a fork of the tree.

It is not uncommon for lions to rob leopards of their kill in this way, but no matter how often we witnessed a lion climbing a tree, they always appeared awkward and out of place.

The next morning we relocated the two male lions in the same area we had left them the night before. Following their fixed stare we saw a lone warthog leaving the safety of his burrow in a termite heap. The hog, oblivious of his hungry onlookers and the impending danger, walked unsuspectingly across the clearing. One lion crouched, then began his hasty stalk. The hog had almost reached the edge of the clearing, when his senses caused him to pause and look back. Three paces and the powerful paw of the lion sent the hog reeling.

The warthog was then grabbed by the throat. Only a squeal was heard from the victim — such had been the speed and precision of the attack.

The hog, oblivious of his hungry onlookers and the impending danger, walked unsuspectingly across the clearing.

The warthog took some ten minutes to die in the grip of the lion — too long a time to wait for his hungry companion, who began eating from the soft flesh of the hog's groin long before the animal had taken his last breath.

Whilst the two males were devouring their prey, the two lionesses arrived and lay back at the edge of the clearing, caution preventing them from approaching. Eventually one female gathered enough courage to move forward, sliding slowly on her belly towards the meat. Suddenly the lion turned on the lioness, teeth bared, lashing out at her with his front paws. Submissively she rolled onto her back whilst cheekily grabbing a scrap-a-leg.

In this case only the one lioness was able to climb the very upright marula tree and she ate what was left of the leopard's kill.

Lions are opportunists and will scavenge meat wherever possible.

65

The lions had been lying up on a termite heap when the warthog unwittingly ventured out of the burrow.

After a short chase the lion delivered a blow to the rump of the warthog bringing it to the ground. As the warthog hit the ground, the lion seized it by the throat and killed it by strangulation.

A young lion surveys the territory but is inexperienced and would most probably spoil the hunt.

Leopard are silent killers, seizing the victim by the throat to eliminate distress calls that may attract other predators that would rob the leopard of its kill.

NewbornCubs

The events I am about to relate occurred
on the third of three trips that I made to the
Sabie Sand area within a six week period.
The object of my endeavours was to locate two new-
born leopard cubs. I was very anxious to
photograph them, but they were
proving to be elusive. A high level of lion
and hyena activity had made the
anxious leopardess move ground, hiding
her precious cubs in inaccessible
places.

... Newborn cubs contd.

During a night drive my persistent search was rewarded when we found both leopardess and her cubs in a tree. We located them by sitting patiently for at least half an hour in the area in which they were last seen. This might not seem long, but in the bush at night there is little to relieve the intense concentration of eyes and ears straining to pierce the velvet darkness. When our patience had almost been stretched to the limit, we suddenly heard a thud probably not more than fifteen metres in front of us. When the headlights were turned on, we found that the noise had been made by a duiker carcass falling out of a tree. The carcass was quickly retrieved by the leopardess who took it back into the tree.

Within a few moments of the leopardess retrieving her kill we were startled by the distressed squeal of a warthog, and hastened to locate the source of the noise. The cause of the warthog's acute distress was the fourteen-month old leopard, our 'juvenile delinquent' friend referred to previously. He had the warthog by the throat and was making a determined, if inexperienced attempt to strangle his prey. After ten minutes he released his grip, but the hog started moving, causing the young leopard to continue with his efforts. It was a painful thirty minutes before the warthog died. During this time the leopard's mother came to lie near the kill, apparently maintaining a maternal interest in the abilities of her offspring. The adolescent cub resented this intrusion, and continuously snarled at his mother who, eventually bored with the affair, returned to her cubs.

This young leopard certainly is a character keeping many delighted game watchers amused for hours. He is quite relaxed in the presence of vehicles and displays all the qualities of a good comedian.

As the mother left the scene, we heard a hyena call. This prompted the leopard to take the warthog into the tree. He managed well enough until he got to the first fork, where he found his path blocked by a broken branch. After a great deal of tugging to force his way through, he lost his grip and unceremoniously fell to the ground with his kill. Looking up into the tree in utter disgust and amazement, he eventually regained his composure and proceeded to disembowel the hog, eating some of the soft flesh in the groin. As the carcass was now lighter, we thought he would attempt to return it to the tree but no such luck. After satisfying his appetite, he lay down contentedly and fell asleep.

We headed back to the tree where we had left the mother leopard, but she had departed and only the duiker carcass was visible.

Early the next morning we returned to the scene of the warthog kill and found the leopard lying on top of his kill which he had by then moved to the fork of a tree. This young leopard certainly was a character keeping many delighted game watchers amused for hours. He was quite relaxed in the presence of vehicles and displayed all the qualities of a good comedian.

After a short time, the leopard left the tree and lay down quietly. This was our cue to leave him and start the search for the mother leopard and her cubs. We found her walking along the bank of a dry river bed, carrying what was left of the duiker kill. Following her for about two

... Newborn cubs contd

kilometres we were rewarded with a good view of her delightful seven-week-old cubs. She gave the meat to the cubs to eat, but although they smelt it, they were not interested. For the following few hours, we watched in pure delight as the cubs played and explored the terrain.

The male cub was extremely adventurous, wandering quite far from his mother. This was dangerous as cubs of this age are vulnerable to hyena, lion, birds of prey and numerous other dangers. The mother was extremely protective, snarling warnings at us to keep our distance.

The mother leopard was slowly being pushed south of her territory by a three-year-old leopardess, who was successfully attempting to enlarge her own territory. Ironically, the three-year-old leopardess was an offspring of her victim. The mother leopard was, in turn, re-establishing herself in territory vacated when a six-year-old leopardess and her cub had died of mange.

Leaving the mother and her cubs we headed west along a dry river bed and were lucky enough to pick up lion spoor. Our tracker informed us that the spoor indicated the presence of a lioness and a single cub in the vicinity. They invited me to accompany them as they tracked the lions. As we walked cautiously through the bush, I marvelled once more at how wise in the ways of the bush trackers are, picking up the slightest trace of a track — even to a toe-print.

A dominant lion, on taking over a territory, will kill the cubs of the area so that the female will come into oestrus and sire a new leader, thus introducing new, male genes into the pride.

We pushed forward, anxiously peering ahead in eager anticipation of locating the lioness and her cub. The bush rustled some distance ahead of us and as we looked up we saw the rear end of a lion disappearing into the thicket. Knowing now where to locate them, we returned to our vehicle and drove into the area. Our lioness and her nine-week old cub were lying at the edge of a thicket on the banks of the river-bed. The lioness was old and scarred and had lost the vision in her left eye. As we studied the pair closely, it became obvious that the cub adored its mother, and the affection radiating from the cub's face was heart-warming to see.

It is interesting to note that the mortality rate amongst lion cubs is approximately fifty percent, depending on the area and the time of year. A dominant lion, on taking over a territory, will kill the cubs of the area so that the female will come into oestrus and sire a new leader, thus introducing new, male genes into the pride.

A huge black-maned lion held the territory to the south-east of the Sabie Sand for some time. This magnificent animal gave us many terrifying experiences. He had the somewhat disturbing habit of charging vehicles and, on occasion, colliding with them. This lion was eventually shot by a local farmer, causing havoc among the lion population in the area. A dominant male brings stability to an area because he chases off any opposition. Without such a leader the members of the pride

.... Newborn cubs contd.

face the threat of an intruder either killing or chasing them off. After the death of the big black-maned lion, his pride of twenty three split up, never to regroup again. So before hunters 'bag' the 'big one', they should think about the consequences.

We returned to the Sabie Sand area two weeks later, and were pleased to find our leopardess and cubs in good health. That evening they came across three hyena, and the mother and cubs beat a hasty retreat into a tree. The mother sat growling at the hyena who kept their distance and then gave up and departed.

The next morning we found two three-year old lions sitting sniffing the wind. The strong wind was probably blowing the smell of the other pride of lions in the area towards them. We waited for nearly two hours in case the two prides should meet, but this was one of those frustrating times in the bush when the hoped-for drama didn't take place.

It was my first sighting of the two seven-week-old leopard cubs. The female bears from one to three cubs after a gestation period of about 105 days.

In the early stages of their lives, their mother may move them to a new shelter every few days.

The female cub was the less adventurous of the two. This factor proved to save her life a few months later.

The cub was the only survivor of the litter and adored its mother. The lioness was battle-scarred and old and we prayed that the cub would survive to adulthood.

The young leopard was inexperienced and it took him 30 minutes to kill this warthog.
By morning he had dragged his kill up to the safety of a tree.

The morning breeze carried the scent of the two dominant lions.

The leopard peered up into the tree reassuring himself that his kill was lodged securely.

The six-year-old leopard and her cub had contracted mange and died three weeks after this picture was taken.

The young male leopard frequented the same territory as his mother but was coming into conflict with the territorial male.

The cubs were chased up a tree by hyena and they remained there until danger had passed.

The buffalo had been wallowing in the mud and looked like a clay statue.

Leopard

During December we returned to Sabie Sand to investigate the progress of the leopard cubs, now four-and-a-half months old.

On our first night drive we found the youngsters safely located on a woodpile, a really good spot if lion or hyena showed their faces. The cubs were alone and we assumed that the mother had gone hunting. Having parked our vehicle near the woodpile, we were pleased to note that the cubs were quite relaxed, in fact the male came closer to investigate our intrusion.

...Leopard contd.

They had grown considerably in the four weeks that had passed since we saw them last. By now they had developed distinctly individual characters. The male was more boisterous, annoying the female as he tugged and pushed her around. He did not retract his claws, and occasionally seemed to inflict pain as he dug them into her.

By the following morning they had left the area and we picked up their tracks, and those of the mother leopard, leading north. After tracking them unsuccessfully for a considerable time we allowed our attention to be diverted by the other game in the area, and this occupied us for the rest of the morning. Having stopped for an early lunch, we started our afternoon drive earlier than usual to continue the search for the leopardess and her cubs. After more unsuccessful tracking and much speculation as to where they might be, we left the area in the golden glow of the late afternoon to drive south, following up on reports of mating lions.

On our arrival in the area, we found a pride consisting of a large black-maned lion, and two lionesses. The second lion, although fully grown, had a small mane and proved to be the subordinate of the two males. After ten minutes, the lioness lying with the subordinate male walked across to the dominant black-maned lion and enticed him to copulate with her. Some twenty minutes later she approached him again. During the mating process the other lioness started moving towards the subordinate lion. The dominant lion instantly abandoned the amorous female and rushed to the second lioness, preventing her from approaching him.

The dominant lion instantly abandoned the amorous female and rushed to the second lioness, preventing her from approaching him.

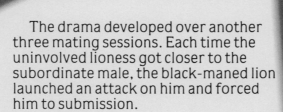

The drama developed over another three mating sessions. Each time the uninvolved lioness got closer to the subordinate male, the black-maned lion launched an attack on him and forced him to submission.

Although the female snarled and showed aggression, she too was finally submissive. The subordinate lion made off and lay up some 40 metres away.

This, however, did not deter the lioness, and each time the male tried to mate with the object of his affections, she tried to move off. The black-maned lion mounted the submissive female eight times over a period of two hours, but only climaxed the first time, the other seven being interrupted by chasing after the second female to keep her from making contact with the subordinate lion.

The culmination of the story came two nights later when we came across the black-maned lion with three lionesses. Two of the lionesses were those observed in our original contact, now joined by a third. The pride was known to Richard our tracker, who informed us that the females were mother and daughters.

The lion mated twice with both daughters in the first hour and although the mother showed some aggression, it was obvious that although she had not come into oestrus, she was due very soon.

The next morning we found the leopardess and her cubs. Following them, we spent four enchanting hours as their mother hunted while the cubs playfully,

... Leopard contd.

but cautiously, followed. Each time the mother started to stalk prey, the cubs would hold back allowing her to hunt on her own.

That evening we found a dead impala lamb lodged in a tree. We waited for nearly an hour for the leopardess to return, but to no avail. Considerable hyena activity in the area was the most likely reason for the non-appearance of the leopardess and her cubs.

During the evening of the next day we located a pride of two adult females and five sub-adult lion. Two of the sub-adult females had found tortoises and, after much difficulty, the one female managed to break a shell by biting through it. I have, on numerous occasions, seen lions trying to bite through a tortoise shell, but this was the first time I had seen one actually succeed. The lioness left the tortoise after rather unsuccessfully trying to eat some of the flesh. As she had only been able to break the top part of the shell, she was unable to gain access to the succulent flesh.

At nightfall the lions began their hunt, attempting unsuccessfully to dig a warthog out of a burrow. At ten o'clock they crossed the break into another property into which we were denied access. This was a good enough reason to return to camp to the seclusion of the boma and a delicious meal enjoyed in cordial company.

This gave me time to reflect on the future of the leopard cubs. They were now adept at climbing trees, although never completely safe from the dangers of the bush. I hoped that they would grow up safely as they had become an important part of my quest to study the leopard.

The mother leopard had gone hunting and left the cubs in the safety of a woodpile.

The male leopard cub was boisterous and seemed, on occasions, to hurt his sister with his unretracted claws.

The mother leopard had climbed a tree from which she was surveying the land.

The male cub was playful and aggravated his mother.

The mother leopard was recognisable by the scar on her nose and a nitch in her ear.

A bond is formed by the cubs but is soon broken when they gain independence.

I had, on previous occasions, seen lions attempting to break through tortoise shells, but this was the first time that I had seen them succeed.

The young lions took turns at trying to get to the succulent meat but soon they became bored.

A playful tap on the nose indicated that the lioness wanted a share in the tortoise.

Lions feed on a wide variety of mammals — from insects to rodents and reptiles, from birds to buffalo.

The lionesses were in oestrus and the dominant lion was determined to keep them both for himself.

When the lioness eventually reached the subordinate lion, the dominant male became aggressive.

The male leopard cub was more adventurous than the female and wandered far off from his mother and sister on numerous occasions.
Although extremely adaptable, leopards are secretive animals and prefer the cover of thick bush.

Savuti

We flew into Savuti on a hot, dusty Sunday in September at the peak of the dry season. At this time of year when water is scarce it is either pumped from boreholes or transported by truck to two water points at the edge of the dry marshland. The vital liquid creates a centre of activity for those animals which have not joined the migratory herds of zebra, wildebeest and buffalo seeking a more life-sustaining habitat. The amount of prey available to be hunted by hungry predators is limited. Large prides of lion very often split up into smaller groups because of the increased competition for meat caused by the larger prey migrating to the north.

...Savuti contd.

Penetrating fine dust blows across the open plains and temperatures soar to sweltering heights. The few pans attract many elephant, and these great grey thirsty fellows push water resources to the limit.

Our first close encounter with elephant bulls (the huge animals were not more than a few metres away), was awesome to say the least, but we soon learned to be at ease with elephant at close quarters.

The water hole at Lloyd's camp in Savuti has two hides which position you so close to the elephants, that you can almost reach out and touch their trunks as they drink. A favourite pastime for game-watchers is to sit quietly on top of the hide, and watch in awe as the usually peaceful beasts push and shove each other, competing for water. On a few occasions we were forced to retreat rather hurriedly as an elephant flicked its trunk at us. Elephants in Savuti are reasonably tolerant of man as man does not hunt them in this environment.

On our arrival at the tented camp I immediately felt the freedom of Africa. Elephant stood peacefully in the shade no more than twenty metres away. This exciting camp brings one as close as possible to the pulsating, stark-reality of the wilds of Africa.

The afternoon drive took us through rocky hills rising out of an ancient lake bed, through heavy sandveld and mopani forests, to open marshland and acacia savannah. Here is a variety of scenery and vegetation rich enough to continually hold one's interest.

On a few occasions we were forced to retreat rather hurriedly as an elephant flicked its trunk at us.

Shortly after arriving at the now dry marsh — the main object of our drive — we located a pride of seven lionesses lazing in the shade of an acacia tree. I was immediately impressed by the size of the Botswana lions which are noticeably larger than their relatives further south. After leaving them to their afternoon relaxation, we came across a pride of twenty lions made up of eight adult females and twelve cubs, each three-to-four months old. We were told that this pride often numbers as many as thirty-six lions.

The signs of competition for meat were clearly visible because the cubs were in poor condition. As the sun dropped towards the western horizon there was none of that frolicking or boisterous play that one expects from cubs at this time of day. Instead they lay in the shade conserving the little energy that the limited food had generated.

Towards sunset the adults moved to the edge of the marshland to look for any prey that could be hunted when darkness fell, and we started to respond to the call of a camp fire dinner.

On our journey back to camp the sunset provided a superb backdrop for photographing elephant — the huge shapes etched in silhouette against the flame-red African sky.

Once again I experienced the wonderful feeling of contentment of being in the heart of a game area with wildlife enthusiasts. After dinner, while wearily sitting around the camp fire, we were entertained by the 'stereo sounds' of the bush at night.

...Savuti contd.

Early on our drive the following day, we were lucky enough to encounter two magnificent lions in the marshland near the first of two waterholes. If life at Savuti at that time of year hinged on the survival of the fittest, these two lions had no problems, being obviously well-fed, sleek and content. As an elephant walked close by, one lion opened a lazy eye. Seeing nothing in the elephant's demeanour to cause concern, he regally turned away and ignored it. When the elephant reached the waterhole he displayed his disgust at the muddy pools by sucking the mud into his trunk and spraying it out again. After three such displays of bad temper, he gave up in total frustration and left the scene.

On the southern side of the marsh we came across large numbers of tsessebe with their hartebeest-like appearance. They seemed to favour the fringes of the woodland where they could combine shade with an open vista. Tsessebe are considered to be a rare species, but they certainly occur in vast numbers at Savuti. In the late evening they moved into open marshlands as these areas offer little cover for predators.

The varied Savuti landscape supports a diverse population of animals. Hunters and hunted are found here, grazers, browsers, anteaters, insect feeders, rodent feeders and carnivore all have their place in the wildlife ecology of Savuti as drama after drama is played out.

As the warthog reached his burrow two hyena grabbed his rear-legs and pulled him out.

The following morning we came upon a lioness who had been bitten across the rear of her spine and could hardly walk. Further on we found two lions, the one digging into warthog burrows. A wound on his right shoulder indicated that he had possibly been in conflict with the injured lioness during the night. He eventually gave up his search for food and lay with his companion who licked him affectionately.

At the edge of the marsh, some way from the injured lions, we found a group of ten hyena lying up in an area which had become known as 'warthog alley'. The hyena were alert; showing a lot of patient interest and we decided to wait. After an hour-and-a-half the hyena spotted a large warthog crossing the marshland. With a total lack of stealth or any apparent awareness of danger, the hyena ran forward, but the warthog spotted them and backtracked when they were some way off. Instead of following a straight course and putting as much ground as possible between himself and the hyena, he turned to his right giving the hyena a chance to close in. Now, obviously making for his burrow, the hog turned right again giving the hyena an even better chance of cutting him off.

As the warthog reached his burrow two hyena grabbed his rear-legs and pulled him out. The unfortunate hog was at bay and, try as he would, he could not defend himself against the hyena onslaught. But he did manage to gore one hyena rather badly on the rump. The ensuing drama was totally one-sided and typically gruesome. Most of the hyena

...Savuti contd.

packed in and attacked the hog's rump, ripping the soft flesh away. Two stayed in front of the hog, distracting him by grabbing at his ears and tusks, the hog all the while squealing for all it was worth. He weakened quickly as the hyena ripped away at flesh, gulping it down in chunks. Mercifully, it died as the hyena continued their gory task, delving deep into the carcass for meat and pulling their heads out dripping with blood.

The hyena is a merciless killer. During the warthog kill, they wailed and chuckled in ghoulish excitement. Not an incident to witness for those with a faint heart or weak stomach.

During the kill, the hyena had been warily looking about — no doubt fearing that lions would be attracted by the noise. Already jackal had gathered at the kill and were foraging for scraps. The hyenas' worst fears were confirmed as two lionesses came bounding towards them. Grabbing a final mouthful the hyenas made off in haste. The lionesses were joined by the rest of the pride of about twenty and it wasn't long before cubs and adults were noisily fighting for a share of the spoils. These seemingly docile beasts turned into savage creatures as they competed for the meagre remains of the warthog, the one lioness closing the incident by making off with the carcass.

In many ways, although my description and photographs may sound and appear gruesome, the warthog was killed by the hyena in a far more efficient manner than I have witnessed with lion kills. The time taken was far shorter and even lion will start eating before the poor victim is dead. Warthog are

extremely tough and a mature male lion can take as long as ten minutes to strangle a large hog.

The pictures of the hyena-kill are far from attractive, but this is the harsh reality of nature and an accurate depiction of survival in the bush. My photographs are made all the more unusual by being taken during the day. Hyena are most active after dark. Although shocking, the photographs add to the visual record of hyena behaviour.

Hyenas have a reputation for being cowardly scavengers, but this is not true. In fact, in certain areas, they hunt and kill seventy percent of their prey. If you take the time to study them, they take on a new face. It is certainly not an attractive one, but extremely interesting nevertheless.

These predators are fascinating animals who have a remarkable social system. To witness them in action was an unforgettable experience. Their speed (in excess of 50 km/h) and their extreme efficiency during the kill ensure that they remain high on the list of survivors in the bush.

We left Savuti knowing that we must return during November to witness the migration of the herd-animals and the dropping of the new-born. A time of great beauty but also of harshness as predators have a royal feast.

Affection is shown towards all cubs in the pride except during competition for food during lean periods.

During the dry period even small tit-bits are of vital importance.

Tsessebe are rarely found in forested areas but frequently occur on the fringes of woodland areas where they have shade and open grasslands for grazing.

Once the chase is on hyena literally 'fly' along at 50 km/h which they can maintain for up to five kilometres.

The hyena's method of killing is by dismembering and tearing his quarry apart which is seemingly vicious and painful, but in many cases much quicker than strangulation.

We must guard against transferring our human emotions and values to wild animals and the natural devices they employ to survive.

Hyena are extremely efficient predators in their own right and in some areas kill up to 70% of their own prey.

Their jaws, and teeth in particular, are well adapted to splintering and crushing even the toughest bones, or shearing through sinew and hide.

As is often the case when other predators have kills, lions take over the meat, because they are stronger. Lions have a keen sense of hearing and, particularly during the dry period, are opportunists.

109

The lions were soon joined by the rest of the pride as hyena and jackal wait close by for scraps.

The hyena stay in close proximity knowing that the lions are only interested in the meat.

Competition for meat is closely contested by all predators.

When times are hard and a large pride is very hungry, there are violent fights over meat.

Possession of meat is normally respected, but circumstances certainly change during lean periods.

Cubs are severely reprimanded by the lionesses during competition for food.

The two dominant lions of the area strengthen the bond by licking each other.

An elephant bull displays his obvious disapproval of the remnants of this muddy waterhole.

Shaking his bulk in a 'show of muscle', an elephant bull disapproves of our close proximity.

A bush glows in the sunset, reflecting the fiery mood of a lioness, alert and ready for the hunt.

Silhouetted against an African sunset, an elephant makes his way towards the now dry Savuti channel.

Return to Savuti

It was a pleasure to leave the hustle and bustle of the concrete jungle to experience the peace and tranquility of Savuti immediately after the rains. In contrast to our previous experience, we found the countryside green and refreshing. The zebra were there in their thousands and the waterholes all held water. The abundance of water was somewhat shortlived as five days after our arrival, consumption by the numerous zebra herds was causing many of the waterholes to dry up.

... Return to Savuti contd.

Our first afternoon game drive found us back on the now lush Savuti marsh and soon after starting out, we were fortunate enough to locate a pair of mating lions. They had apparently been in the area for three days mating on average every twenty minutes which probably accounted for the couple looking extremely thin and much worse for wear.

Many matings fail to result in fertilisation, in spite of the frequency of copulation. The mating process is dramatically ritualistic. The lioness circles and lies down in front of the lion soliciting him. Copulation is brief and accompanied by loud aggressive behaviour. The lion bites her on the back of the neck as he climaxes, then there is much snarling as the lioness turns on her suitor.

After mating twice in half an hour, it became obvious that the male had had enough and he set out purposefully towards his pride. Walking majestically along the edge of the marsh, he passed flocks of malibu storks which flew up into trees and settled to roost for the night.

Leaving camp at sunrise the following morning, we found a pride of seven lionesses walking along the road. They were watched closely by three hyena who were crunching the bones of a zebra that the lionesses had killed the previous night. The lionesses, in spite of their bloated stomachs, were in high spirits and we were entertained for some time as they romped and played in the fresh morning air.

The lioness circles and lies down in front of the lion soliciting him. Copulation is brief and accompanied by loud aggressive behaviour.

Leaving them to their games, we stopped to watch a dwarf mongoose basking in the sun. In the glow of the morning sunlight we passed by a herd of zebra. Carmine bee-eaters were perching in a dead tree and swooping into the grassland to forage for insects. A vulture flew off as we passed by, to start his daily routine of gliding to great heights on the thermals from where he would scan the countryside below for signs of carrion.

We watched a herd of zebra drinking, noticing that one had been mauled by lions during the night. Although zebra are subject to heavy predation, they defend themselves courageously kicking out with their hooves.

We noticed that the zebra were all looking in the same direction. We drove into the area indicated by the alert zebra to find a pride of lions and cubs with whom we had become acquainted on our previous trip. The cubs which had been in poor condition were in good health and now numbered ten, two of the original twelve either died of starvation or perhaps they were killed by predators. The whole pride, with the exception of one lioness, looked well fed. She was limping and bleeding from a cut on her chest. Perhaps she had been responsible for an encounter with the injured zebra that we had seen earlier. She had been badly hurt and was unable to feed with the rest of the pride.

...Return to Savuti contd.

On our way back to camp we stopped at a waterhole in which a herd of elephant were noisly enjoying a mudbath. We then drove down into a dip so that I could photograph elephant from a dramatic angle — walking on a ridge outlined against the sky. While we were parked to take advantage of this situation, an elephant moved up behind us and trumpeted as he charged our vehicle. I grabbed a camera fitted with a 35mm wide angle lens and photographed madly. We stood our ground and the elephant stopped only a few metres from us. We assumed, and rightly so, that it was only a mock charge mainly with the objective of driving us off or to see to what extent he could get away with 'flexing his muscles'. We were greatly relieved when the elephant retreated and gave us a wide berth.

Back at camp, we were told about a pack of seven wild dogs that had killed an impala. Much to our disappointment we had driven past the area thirty minutes before they appeared, so missing the drama of the hunt.

That afternoon we drove to the area where the wild dogs had last been seen. They looked distinctly overfed and uncomfortable.

The three wild dog pups were playfully tugging at a stick. This interesting animal is, like the jackal, not a true 'dog' because it only has four toes on each foot — lacking the fifth toe or dew claw to be found on all true canines.

While we parked to take advantage of this situation, an elephant moved up behind us and trumpeted as he charged our vehicle.

Unfortunately, many people have a strong dislike of wild dogs due to their apparently bloodthirsty hunting habits and they have been systematically wiped out in some of Africa's reserves.

It is important not to judge the actions of predators by standards based upon our own perspectives and feelings. These animals survive by behaving in the natural way that has evolved over time. In places where they have turned to killing domestic stock, this is usually as a result of man's wanton killing of the game in such areas. Without their natural prey, obviously they will turn to whatever is available in order to survive.

The next day I was obliged to return to the dubious normality of my work environment consoling myself that there would be other opportunities to enjoy photographing the natural wonders of the 11,700 square kilometres of The Chobe National Park, which houses Savuti and some of Africa's most densely populated animal kingdoms.

121

The great size of an elephant makes it impossible for the animal to jump even one centimetre off the ground.

Scent marking demonstrates lions' right to territory so as to warn others off.

Zebra are noisy, restless creatures, and when alarmed or assembling at a drinking place, they constantly utter a characteristic barking whinny.

This zebra showed signs of a close encounter with lion during the previous night.

Elephants occur in great numbers in Botswana and spend much of their time at the waterholes.

Although seemingly bloodthirsty, a wild dog's hunting methods are extremely efficient.

Although the wild dogs had killed an impala ram earlier that day and were uncomfortably overfed, they still found the energy to amuse themselves.

Zebra watch a pride of lion from close quarters, feeling safe as long as they have them in sight.

During the peak of the dry season, the lion cubs are in poor condition as the scarcity of meat begins to take its toll.

Lions have a sensitive olfactory pouch in the roof of their mouths which tells them much about the scents of other lions.

Lion are predominantly nocturnal, with a tendency to be active around sunrise and sunset.

The lioness invites the male by circling, then rolling and crouching in front of him.

The pair may copulate every 20 minutes over a period of five or six days.

The lioness turns on her suitor with bared teeth as he dismounts. He slaps her in retaliation. The aggression continues as both animals bare their teeth and snarl at each other.

Lion prides occupy territories or home ranges which may vary greatly in size depending on local conditions and availability of food.

Lions often rub against each other. This strengthens the pride bond.

The massive skull is reduced in weight by having a honeycomb structure. Males have convex, and females concave foreheads.

During the rut (mating season) the impala rams chase each other about, uttering loud, savage grunting and snorting sounds.

Two elephants make an impressive backdrop as we head back to camp to enjoy the fireside comradeship.

Etosha Pan

My travels in pursuit of varied game drives took me into the harsh, starkly beautiful Namibia area. The vast Etosha Game Reserve is desert-white, arid land which makes you screw up your eyes against the glare. Zebra and wildebeest congregate at the waterholes quenching their thirst, gaining only brief respite from the intense, parching heat. Zebra, in spite of the heat, find the energy to battle for dominance at water-holes, their disturbances sending white puffs of dust into the air.

Etosha may give the impression that it is a parched wasteland during the winter months, but its dry vastness is a hive of activity. Thousands of zebra, wildebeest, springbok and many other species live under the blazing Etosha sun.

... Etosha pan contd.

As we drove along the tourist routes, dust as fine and white as talcum powder rose behind the vehicle like smoke from a steam engine.

Elephant abound in Etosha. There are so many, in fact, that the habitat appears insufficient to support such great numbers. However they only remain in Etosha during the winter months before they migrate to the north. Nature has a chance to "re-stock the larder" during spring, summer and autumn.

The elephant in Etosha are a delight to watch. Almost human in their ways, they can be affectionate, considerate, comical and at times aggressive and moody. Elephants are gregarious, normally forming into family groups of varying numbers. Their family and social structure is not unlike the human species. They do not maintain territories but move over areas determined by the availability of food. At times, when they are subjected to heavy persecution or when migrating from severe drought, groups may amalgamate to form larger herds.

Elephants perform a vital service to other animals in drier areas by locating water and then digging small wells with their trunks and forefeet.

There is nothing more fascinating than watching a herd of elephant arriving at a drinking-place. As they reach the water, prolonged, vibrating, rumbling sounds are interspersed with abrupt squealing sounds, apparently made through the trunk. This symphony is accompanied by the bad-tempered screams of youngsters sparring and quarreling, or angry mothers reproving disobedient infants.

Elephants perform a vital service to other animals in drier areas by locating water and then digging small wells with their trunks and forefeet.

Young elephants gambol and disport themselves like gigantic puppies, playfully chasing other animals within reach. Water drawn up in the trunk is poured down thirsty throats, and after thirsts are quenched the great beasts wade gratefully into the cool depths, sluicing water over their backs. Quite suddenly the herd decides to move. In a moment they shuffle off *en masse* and silence reigns where, a few minutes before, the air resounded with a cacophony of sound.

When they reach puberty young males leave the family group to form a loose association with other males. Really old bulls usually become loners, preferring a solitary existence to the noise and activity of herd life.

Early morning over the north-eastern section of the Etosha Pan, which still held water when I was there, was truly magnificent. As the red glow of sunrise was duplicated in the water, flocks of flamingoes gracefully fed off large organisms and tiny crustaceans. The water mirrored the flamingoes as they flew across the lake on their nomadic route to preferred arid areas with irregular rainfall. Flamingoes are filter-feeders. Necks curved, they swing their heads from side to side as they take in the microscopic morsels.

We drove on along the eastern edge of the pan and saw hyena mating. Both participants seemed totally uninterested in the proceedings, the male yawning from time to time (not very flattering to his mate).

All along the pan, springs rise up. Animals travel great distances to find water as overgrazing near established areas of water creates a shortage of food. The springs further inland seem to hold more water, and are the essence of

... Etosha pan contd.

life for many species. At most springs there is wildlife of all sorts, including squirrel and mongoose which can easily be spotted in the sparse vegetation. The ground-dwelling squirrel is larger and more robust than his tree-dwelling relative. They are easily identifiable with pronounced white stripes along the flank and large bushy tails. The ground-squirrel has adapted well to the hot, semi-arid region and is able to withstand great heat and survive on little water. On very hot days they use their wide tails as umbrellas by curving them over their backs and spreading them out.

As we watched a group of vultures at one waterhole, two lappet-faced vultures came dancing towards us. The lappet-faced vulture is the largest of the species and has a most formidable beak. While watching the vultures we were delighted to be joined by a bateleur eagle who landed nearby to drink. Before long, he was joined by an immature bateleur.

The magificent bateleur eagle is easily recognisable in flight as it rocks from side to side. Hence the French name 'bateleur' meaning 'tight-rope walker'.

As the late afternoon sky in the west turned a deep red, a group of wildebeest moved away from a waterhole, their manes glowing as if on fire.

Driving back to camp, we waited patiently as a herd of elephant passed in front of us, their great ghost-like shapes silhouetted against the Etosha sunset.

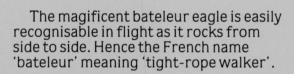

Giraffe have the largest heart in the animal kingdom, enabling them to pump blood some three metres up to the brain.

Burchells zebra are gregarious and live in family groups numbering up to twenty individuals.

In a test of strength, two bulls establish their dominance.

When confronted with danger, springbok will often start 'pronking' and it is from this behaviour that their name is derived.

A fight between two red hartebeest bulls consists of violent pushing and jousting. Injuries are rare and losers flee with the victors in hot pursuit.

An elephant calf indicates her pleasure on arriving at the waterhole by splashing with her trunk.
Small ones gambol and disport like gigantic puppies.

Elephants have a close relationship with their mothers, brothers and sisters.

Young elephants are playful and mischievously inclined, and are often wrongly accused of charging cars in game parks.

E T O S H A   P A N

A zebra drinks at dusk knowing that as night falls he becomes vulnerable to the prowling predators. Rival stallions fight violently, often lacerating each other badly but never fighting to the death.

Lone wildebeest bulls are usually territorial animals and during the mating season they herd the cows into their territory.

A pair of mating hyenas seemingly display boredom during copulation.

The story that elephants go to a 'graveyard' to die is a myth which probably arose from the fact that in the past large numbers of bones have been found together.

A herd of elephants walk into the night as the leaders test the evening breeze.

Death of a Cub

Christmas was over. A trip was to be made a few weeks hence on which I planned to continue my photographic record of the growth of the two leopard cubs.

This was not to be. An unexpected and unwelcome phone call brought news that the male leopard cub of the litter had been killed. So once again, as the harsh realities of nature were brought to mind, I set out to witness the last part of this particular animal story.

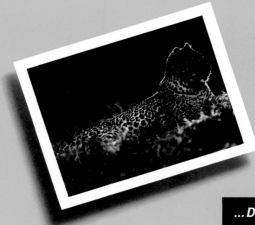

... Death of a cub contd.

I arrived at Sabie Sand early the following morning and was transported to where the dead male cub lay. The mood in the vehicle was quiet and sombre as we sped towards a large leadwood tree where the partly-eaten cub rested in a fork of the branches.

The young male had been by far the most adventurous of the two. The more boisterous, the first to climb a tree, the first to wander off on his own. He had paid the price.

The mother leopard and surviving female cub were also lying in the same tree, keeping watch over the body of the cub. After about an hour both descended from the tree and lay down some twenty metres away. The young female cub was in a playful mood, blisfully oblivious of the distress of her mother. The leopardess, setting aside her sorrow, played with the cub until the effort became too much and she warned it off. This action was followed by her plaintiff calls to her dead cub, over and over again. On two occasions the surviving cub answered by approaching her mother believing them to be for her. Each time she was quickly warned off and retreated in confusion.

Some time later both mother and cub returned to the leadwood tree where the mother, obviously exhausted, fell asleep. This prompted the cub to leave the tree once again and head off in the direction of the river bed. We sat in silence for nearly two hours as the leopardess slept, and we pondered on her next move.

Eventually she awoke, gently picked up her dead cub in her mouth, descended from the tree and carried it into some long grass nearby. Slowly she ate at the remaining meat of the cub.

Eventually she awoke, gently picked up her dead cub in her mouth, descended from the tree and carried it into some long grass nearby. Slowly she ate at the remaining meat of the cub. For the next half-hour we watched her obvious distaste for this procedure. Regularly she would leave the carcass to walk around and issue her pitifull call, twice she rushed towards us warning us away.

It is extremely rare for a predator to eat the flesh of other predators. On a few occasions I have witnessed this particular leopardess kill civet and genet cats who apparently have good-tasting meat, but never has she eaten them. So it is fairly safe to assume that it was neither hunger, nor the lust for meat that caused her to eat the cub.

It is my personal belief that the scene we were watching was a form of burial. Hyena had attempted to take the carcass away from her, and she had fiercely protected the dead cub. Again we drew the comparison between man and leopard as the grieving mother preserved the right to bury, in her way, her child.

Anxious to understand how the untimely death of the young cub had occurred, we set out to look for evidence. Soon we found numerous lion spoor and other small clues from which we could piece together the story.

The mother leopard and her cubs were eating from the carcass of a kill which she had failed to hoist into a tree. Whilst enjoying the meal with her cubs, she had dropped her guard, and the family was surprised by a pride of lion.

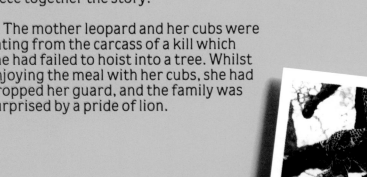

... Death of a cub contd.

It is by no means unusual for predators to kill weaker predators, especially cubs. It is an essential law of survival for a type predator or even opposing prides to eliminate as much competition for meat as possible.

On the four occasions that we have witnessed the death of leopard cubs, each time the mother has eaten the flesh of her offspring. This form of burial, seems to be peculiar only to leopard, as we have no record of other predators following this practice.

We stayed with the mother leopard for five days after the death. Each day her distress was still in evidence as she moved very little and continued her calling for the dead cub. Not once did she attempt to hunt for food for herself or the remaining cub. We quietly left her and, even though she was out of sight, her calls could still be heard. However, we knew that the instinct for survival would overcome her grief and life would go on for her and her cub.

The leopard cub spent a lot of time staring at the remains of her brother.

The mother leopard displayed signs of tremendous grief, lying around protecting the remains of the cub from scavengers.

The leopardess, in spite of her sorrow, played with the cub until the effort became too much.

The cub remained in close proximity to her mother .

During the few days after the death of her brother, the surviving cub showed a lot of affection toward her mother. Our hearts warmed towards the pain in their time of grief.

The mother leopard seemed to have to gather up courage before she could approach her dead cub.

She removed the body from the fork of the tree . . .

. . . then climbed down the tree and ate from the carcass, flinching as she did so. This gesture is evidently a form of burial.

Photographers Notes

My trips to many wildlife areas have been a quest to study the different elements of nature which I cherish and love to photograph. I desire to study nature and convey it through photographs to all who inhabit this earth, and I hope that in some way this will contribute to the conservation of this rapidly diminishing environment.

To obtain photographs of various species from dramatically different angles, I decided to photograph from ground level. My first experience of working in this way was in a private game reserve where one is permitted to leave the vehicle. We were following a pride of five lionesses and stopped the vehicle in a dip. I lay on my stomach a few metres from the vehicle and awaited the approaching lionesses. They were following a game path which I thought they would continue to follow, passing a safe distance from me.

The first lioness to come over the ridge spotted me and stalked towards me. She came within four metres and lay down, watching me intently. The other four lionesses did likewise, and I found myself lying amongst the pride. None of them showed aggression, although they sat watching me intently for some time before they got up and walked away.

I hope that, in some small way, this book will encourage our conservationists to continue their commendable work, and that more people will come to experience and appreciate Africa's wonderful natural heritage.

Gerald Hinde

Acknowledgements

I am indebted to the people who worked so hard and spent so many inconvenient hours in the bush with me. All of you are highly professional, knowledgeable and skilled and I have greatly enjoyed working with you.

At Londolozi, Dave and John Varty were always extremely helpful.

Peter and Yvonne Short on many occasions kept food until the early hours of the morning. Anne Dickson always seemed to manage accommodation. The rangers and trackers went to great lengths to locate and follow predators — sometimes at great personal risk. Special thanks must go to Trevor Lindegger and Richard Siwela. I am also grateful to Elmon Mhlongo, Kimbian Mnisi, Paddy Hagelthorn, Lex Hes, Richard Delarey, Tony Adams, Hugh Marshall and the other rangers and trackers. At Ngala Lodge, Bob Manthe and Darren Saunders were extremely hospitable. We had a kind reception at Thornybush from that colourful character, Frank Dyson.

To the officials of the Botswana, Etosha, Kalahari Gemsbok and Kruger National Parks, I thank you for all your friendly assistance. A special word of thanks to Jan Joubert, Chief public relations officer at Etosha. During our stay at Savuti, Lloyd and June Wilmot and their capable staff were most helpful.

My thanks to Gillian Ballard, Dave Neate and Tim Rowland who were responsible for how this book looks and reads. I acknowledge *'Maberley's Mammals of Southern Africa'* as a reference to various animal behaviours.